Teach Me Piano ™

Interactive multimedia piano-teaching system

You will need the Product ID number from the Registration Card when you install the software. You also will need this number if you phone for technical support. Please copy this number to the line below so you will have it for future reference!

Product ID Number: _____

Teach Me Piano ™

Here's How to Contact Voyetra Technologies

By mail	Voyetra Technologies, Inc. 5 Odell Plaza Yonkers, NY 10701-1406 USA
Fax	914-966-1102
Bulletin Board	914-966-1216 N, 8, 1
CompuServe®	72702.2037
America Online®	voyetra@aol.com
Sales and Information	800-233-9377 (inside USA) 914-966-0600 (outside USA)
Sales	sales@voyetra.com
Information	info@voyetra.com
Technical Support	914-966-0600 support@voyetra.com
Website	http://www.voyetra.com
To Register Software	register@voyetra.com

Registering Your Software

You can register your software by mail, fax, phone, BBS, Internet or WWW.

December 1996 • Part Number: 04840-M01 • ISBN 1-888743-13-1

Introduction

Even If You Don't Read This Manual... Here's What You'll Want to Know!

Everything is just a point-and-click away.
All of the features of Teach Me Piano can be accessed from the main screen. This is referred to as the "Piano Room." Move the mouse pointer around the Piano Room and when the name of the module you would like to open displays on screen, just click!

There's a right-click pop-up menu.
Right-clicking the mouse in the Piano Room displays a pop-up menu from which you can toggle the Teach Me Piano introduction on and off, view information about the program (including the "About" box with the Product ID number) and close the program without the final musical "goodbye."

You will need the Product ID number if you phone for Technical Support. This number can be found in the "About" box, accessible from the right-click pop-up menu.

Online help is always available.
Teach Me Piano has comprehensive online help. Help is always available by clicking the question mark (?) on the bottom right of the Piano Room screen.

If you have been using Voyetra's Discovering Keyboards,™ you can automatically bring your user settings and imported MIDI files over to Teach Me Piano. During installation, a dialog box prompts you that Discovering Keyboards has been detected and asks if you would like to transfer the user data from Discovering Keyboards to Teach Me Piano. For more information, refer to the "Up and Running" chapter of this manual.

You'll need a four-octave MIDI keyboard to fully utilize the program. Teach Me Piano will run without a MIDI keyboard; however, a musical keyboard is necessary for the Keyboard Lessons section of the program. This keyboard needs to contain at least four-octaves in order to play all of the songs and exercises in the program.

If you do not have a keyboard — or the necessary adapter cable — you can order them directly from Voyetra Technologies. (See page *ii* at the front of this manual for information on how to contact us.) Refer to "Setting Up Your MIDI Keyboard" in the "Up and Running" chapter for information on connecting a MIDI keyboard. For information on testing your keyboard's connections, refer to the "MediaCheck" chapter.

Keyboard Lessons will keep track of many students. Your entire family can use Teach Me Piano and the software will maintain individualized records of each user's progress. Just make certain that each user always signs in under his/her own name.

You can jump to any lesson at any time. Although we highly recommend that you move through the lessons in a sequential order, you can always jump to a lesson which covers a specific keyboard-playing technique. Refer to the Appendix at the back of this User's Guide for a complete listing of the topics in Teach Me Piano.

Keyboard Lessons and the Songbook have keyboard shortcut keys. There are a many shortcut keys which make the Keyboard Lessons and Songbook sections of the program easier to use. A listing of these appears in the "Quick Overview" chapter.

You can skip the opening introduction. To interrupt the opening Introduction and go directly to the Piano Room, click ESC while the Introduction is playing.

You can import your own MIDI files into the Songbook ...

and then print them out complete with note-names. Refer to the "Songbook" chapter for more information.

You can practice or perform any song at any time.

When you are in the Songbook, you can switch to either the Trainer Screen, to practice the song, or the Performance Screen, to perform the song with background accompaniment. Then, when you are in the Performance Screen, you can go to either the Trainer Screen or back to the Songbook. Refer to the "Songbook" chapter for more information.

You can adjust the volume in Keyboard Lessons.

If you find that the volume is too loud or too soft in Keyboard Lessons, use the Performance Options dialog box — click on the "Metronome" at the bottom of the screen — to adjust it. Refer to the "Keyboard Lessons" chapter for details.

Acknowledgments

Many thanks to the talented people who helped create this User's Guide.

Ms. Ronni Geist
Documentation Manager

Technical Writing/Editing
Michael P. Constantino
Robert Goodman

Acrobat File Creation
Keith Nitsch

Graphics
Carlos Crespo
Keith Nitsch
Scott Walters

Table of Contents

Chapter I

Getting Started...

Welcome!

Thank you for purchasing Teach Me Piano! This program is one of Voyetra Technologies' CD-ROM titles designed to bring educational and entertaining music products to multimedia computer users.

Voyetra Technologies has been in the business of music hardware and software for more than 20 years. We are a leading supplier of programming, engineering services, and software applications to the PC and multimedia industries.

Our software is included with many of the sound cards sold today, so there is a good chance you already own some of our other products.

Whether you are a new acquaintance or a Voyetra veteran, you will benefit from our long-standing upgrade policy and our excellent technical support.

As a registered user, you are entitled to special discounts on our other products — but we can't offer you these benefits if we don't know who you are! So before you install Teach Me Piano, take a minute to register your software. And welcome to the Voyetra family!

Benefits of Registering Your Software

There are many benefits to registering your software. In addition to our limited warranty, you'll also receive:

- **Update Notifications** — we'll keep you informed of software updates and new Voyetra products.

- **VoyeTracks™ Newsletter** — we'll let you know about developments at Voyetra Technologies, with information on how others are using our software and tips to help you get the most from our products.

- **Upgrade Plan** — we'll offer you discounts on Voyetra's full-featured PC sound products.

- **Technical Support** — we'll be happy to help you get your software installed before you register; however, you must be a registered user to receive full technical support.

Here's How to Register

Mail	Voyetra Technologies 5 Odell Plaza Yonkers, NY 10701-1406 USA
Fax	914.966.1102
Phone	800.233.9377 (inside USA) 914.966.0600 (outside USA)
Bulletin Board	914.966.1216 N, 8, 1
World Wide Web	http://www.voyetra.com
Internet	register@voyetra.com

 You can register your software by mail, fax, phone, BBS, Internet or World Wide Web — whichever is easiest for you.

What You'll Need to Run the Software

All of your multimedia hardware and software should be working correctly *before* you install the software. If your system isn't working properly, neither will Teach Me Piano!

- You must have Microsoft Windows (3.1 or 95) installed and working on your computer.

- You must have an external MIDI controller (keyboard), with four or more octaves, to play all of the songs in Keyboard Lessons. For songs at the beginning of the program, a smaller MIDI keyboard is acceptable. A MIDI keyboard is NOT required for the other applications in Teach Me Piano.

- You must have headphones and/or speakers connected to the jack labeled "output" or "speakers" on the back of your sound card. If you are using speakers, they need to have their own amplification since the output from the sound card may be too low to power them. Speakers with built-in amps are powered either by battery or AC.

Video Playback

Teach Me Piano utilizes the full capabilities of a high-end multimedia PC. As with all sophisticated multimedia programs, the more robust your computer system, the better and faster the software will perform. This is especially true for video playback. On older, slower systems, the quality of the videos may be poor, the audio and video may be out of sync and the program may run slowly.

 To free up system resources and improve performance, close down any other applications before running Teach Me Piano.

Minimum Hardware Requirements

Listed below are the *minimum* hardware requirements for Teach Me Piano.

IBM PC or compatible with 486DX2/66MHz or higher processor	Since Teach Me Piano makes full use of the multimedia capabilities of a PC, a Pentium® system is highly recommended. On a 486, the software will run extremely slowly.
8 megabytes of RAM (Random Access Memory)	Teach Me Piano will NOT run with less than 8 megabytes of RAM. Additional RAM — beyond 8 MB — will improve the performance of multimedia applications on your PC.
SVGA monitor and adapter capable of displaying at least 256 colors	Teach Me Piano was designed to run in 256 colors or more.
Hard disk drive with at least 6 megabytes of storage space available	Although the program runs off the CD-ROM, 6 megabytes are required to install Video for Windows, which is necessary for viewing the videos.
Double-speed (or faster) CD-ROM drive	A double-speed CD-ROM drive is the minimum. A faster CD-ROM drive will improve performance.
16-bit Windows-compatible sound card	Because all of the .WAV files are recorded in 16-bit, a 16-bit sound card is required. A wavetable sound card will significantly increase the sound quality of the MIDI music in Teach Me Piano's applications. This is particularly true of the keyboard (piano) sounds.
Four-octave MIDI keyboard	A four-octave MIDI-compatible keyboard is needed to play all the songs and exercises in the Keyboard Lessons section. For the earlier lessons, a smaller keyboard is acceptable.

What's Included in Teach Me Piano

Teach Me Piano provides a full course of piano lessons. With a MIDI keyboard connected to your PC, the interactive scoring system evaluates your performance so you can see how you are progressing. Coupled with videos, animations and colorful illustrations, Teach Me Piano makes learning to play the piano easy and fun! Here are the applications you'll find in Teach Me Piano:

- **Keyboard Lessons**
  This is the main component. Divided into six sections with more than 150 lessons, Keyboard Lessons presents the full spectrum of keyboard-playing skills including note-reading in the treble and bass clefs, rhythm and timing, finger numbers and finger positions, key signatures, time signatures, scales and chords. Teach Me Piano can maintain records for many students, so all of the members of your family can start at their own levels and proceed at their own rates.

- **Musician's Reference**
  An introduction to musical notation, the Musician's Reference contains easy-to-understand definitions, colorful diagrams, and illustrations to explain commonly-used musical terms.

- **Songbook**
  Use the Songbook to organize — by Title, Style, Composer, or Level of Difficulty — the more than 75 songs that come with Teach Me Piano. Choose a song and go either to the Trainer Screen to practice it or to the Performance Screen to play it with full background accompaniment. You can even import your own MIDI files into the Songbook and then print them out as sheet music, complete with note names.

- **MediaCheck™**
  This multimedia diagnostic utility provides a quick and easy way to test and troubleshoot the multimedia components on your computer. A series of displays takes you through the testing process.

Teach Me Piano's Relationship to Discovering Keyboards

Some users of Teach Me Piano may also be owners of Voyetra's Discovering Keyboards.™ If you have been using Discovering Keyboards, you will notice a similarity between the two products.

Discovering Keyboards was designed as an introductory piano course. In addition to beginning piano lessons and the *Songbook*, Discovering Keyboards also includes the *Keyboard Tour* — a multimedia history of keyboard instruments, *Understanding MIDI and Synthesis* — a multimedia overview of PC sound technology, and the *Game Room* — three, fun, arcade-style games which test musical knowledge.

Teach Me Piano, on the other hand, was designed as a comprehensive piano-teaching course. It contains beginner through intermediate keyboard lessons, the *Songbook*, and the *Musician's Reference* — a guide to the basics of musical notation.

Although Teach Me Piano can be used as a standalone product, it also can be used as an upgrade to Voyetra's Discovering Keyboards, since it continues on with three additional sections of lessons, advancing the user from beginner through intermediate playing techniques.

If you are a Discovering Keyboards user, Sections 1, 2, and 3 of the Keyboard Lessons in Teach Me Piano will be familiar to you. They are the same lessons you studied in Discovering Keyboards.

You may wonder, "Why this overlap of content?" The answer is simple. We, at Voyetra, believe that Discovering Keyboards users who purchase Teach Me Piano will find that having the entire course of study on a single CD-ROM makes using the Keyboard Lessons in Teach Me Piano much easier and more convenient.

Since Keyboard Lessons can track the progress of many users, when family members are working on different sections of the program — for example, if little Johnny is just beginning Section 1, while Mom is practicing Section 4 — having the entire course of study on a single CD means that there is no need to swap discs back-and-forth between Discovering Keyboards and Teach Me Piano when each of them wants to practice.

Discovering Keyboards™

Keyboard Tour™	
Understanding MIDI & Synthesis™	
Music Games™	
SoundCheck™	
Songbook	

Teach Me Piano™

Sections

1	4
2	5
3	6

Musician's Reference

MediaCheck™

Songbook

Sections 1, 2, and 3 are included in both Discovering Keyboards and Teach Me Piano.

The Keyboard Tour™ and Understanding MIDI & Synthesis™ are also available on the Multimedia History of Music Keyboards™ with Introduction to MIDI™ Value CD.

Music Games™ is also available on the Multimedia Music Games™ Value CD.

 For a complete listing of the course of study in the Keyboard Lessons, refer to "Keyboard Lessons' Content" in the Appendix at the back of this book.

Similarly, users advancing from Section 3 (the last section in Discovering Keyboards) into Section 4 (the first section in Teach Me Piano), will have a smoother transition, since they can seamlessly move back-and-forth between these sections on one disc — the Teach Me Piano disc.

Additionally, having the entire course of study on a single CD-ROM means that when you advance to Sections 4 through 6, you can always go back to an earlier section when you want to review an earlier lesson, and the songs you have learned to play will always be available when you want to perform them in the Performance Hall.

And finally, the look-and-feel of the two products are similar. Since all of your user information and imported MIDI files are transferred automatically from Discovering Keyboards to Teach Me Piano during the installation of the software, moving from Discovering Keyboards into Teach Me Piano should be a very comfortable experience.

Keyboard Tour, MIDI and Synthesis, and Games

If you are a Teach Me Piano user who wants to learn more about the history of musical keyboards and how computers make music — or who wants to enjoy several games to improve note reading and rhythm skills — you can either purchase these applications separately, on Voyetra's Value CDs, or you can buy Discovering Keyboards, which contains all of these modules and the first three sections of Keyboard Lessons in one easy-to-use software package. See page *ii* of this manual for information on how to contact Voyetra.

Working with Windows

Teach Me Piano works with Microsoft Windows. To use Teach Me Piano, you should know how to:

- Use the mouse to move the cursor, select items, click, double-click and drag.
- Work buttons, drop-down lists and other controls that appear on Windows screens.
- Find, open, name, save and close files.

If any of these techniques are unfamiliar to you, refer to your Windows manual or work through the tutorial included with Windows before you proceed.

Chapter 2

Up and Running

Installing Teach Me Piano

Teach Me Piano has an automatic installation process.

To install the software:

1. Make certain you have the Product ID number. (This can be found on the Registration Card.)
2. Place the CD in your computer's CD-ROM drive.
3. For Windows 3.1, choose Run from the Program Manager's File menu. For Windows 95, choose Run from the Taskbar's Start menu. (When you insert the Teach Me Piano disc for the first time in Windows 95, you are automatically prompted to Run it.)
4. In the Run dialog box, type the letter name of the drive followed by **\setup**. If your CD-ROM drive is d:, type **d:\setup**
5. Press Enter.
6. Follow the on-screen instructions.

 During installation, Indeo video drivers must be installed. If you view the Indeo README file during the install, it will appear as though you quit Teach Me Piano's installation prematurely — before it was complete. However, this is not the case. Teach Me Piano will fully install.

If You've Been Using Discovering Keyboards

When you install Teach Me Piano, if Discovering Keyboards has been installed on your system, a dialog box informs you that Discovering Keyboards has been detected and asks if you would like to transfer the user data from Discovering Keyboards to Teach Me Piano.

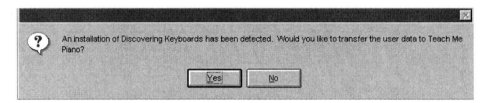

- If you choose "Yes," all the user data will be placed into Teach Me Piano. This lets you continue with your lessons from where you left off in Discovering Keyboards. Choosing "Yes" also transfers over any MIDI song files you may have imported into the Discovering Keyboards' Songbook.

- If you choose "No," none of the data will be transferred to Teach Me Piano.

README File

During installation, a README file may be installed. This file contains important information that was not available when this manual was printed. Be sure to read this information before you proceed. You might also want to print this file and keep it for future reference.

To view the README file:

1. Double-click on the README icon.
2. In Windows 3.1, Windows Write will open and display the file. In Windows 95, WordPad will open and display the file.
3. To print the README file, choose Print from the File menu of either Windows Write or WordPad.

Running Teach Me Piano

Teach Me Piano works both with Windows 3.1 (or later) and with Windows 95. You must have the disc in the CD-ROM drive to run the program.

To run Teach Me Piano from Windows 3.x:

- Double-click on the Teach Me Piano icon in the Voyetra Teach Me Piano program group.

To run Teach Me Piano from Windows 95:

- Click Start. Point to Programs. Point to Voyetra Teach Me Piano. Click on the Teach Me Piano icon.

  When you insert Teach Me Piano for the first time in Windows 95, you are automatically prompted to Run it.

 If you have any problems with the audio or video portions of the software, refer to the Troubleshooting section in the Appendix of this User's Guide.

Setting Up Your MIDI Keyboard

A MIDI synthesizer or MIDI keyboard is required to fully-utilize the Keyboard Lessons and Songbook. This keyboard must be at least four-octaves long in order to play all of the exercises and songs. A musical keyboard is not required for the Musician's Reference.

To connect a MIDI keyboard, you will need a MIDI adapter cable. If you do not have a MIDI adapter cable attached to your keyboard, don't despair. You can still use the software and learn how to play a keyboard instrument. However, Teach Me Piano will not be able to evaluate your progress unless you have this cable.

If you need a cable — or a MIDI keyboard — you can purchase one at your local computer store or order one directly from Voyetra. (See page *ii* at the front of this manual for information on how to contact Voyetra Technologies.)

Making the Connections

The following illustration describes how to connect the MIDI cable.

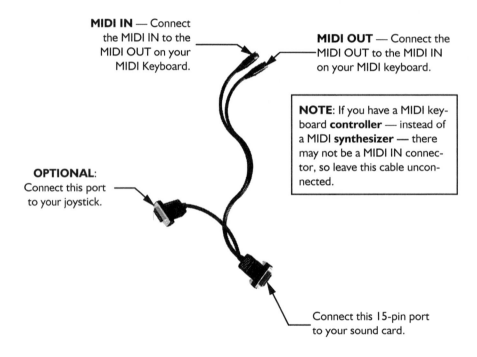

MIDI IN — Connect the MIDI IN to the MIDI OUT on your MIDI Keyboard.

MIDI OUT — Connect the MIDI OUT to the MIDI IN on your MIDI keyboard.

NOTE: If you have a MIDI keyboard **controller** — instead of a MIDI **synthesizer** — there may not be a MIDI IN connector, so leave this cable unconnected.

OPTIONAL: Connect this port to your joystick.

Connect this 15-pin port to your sound card.

 To view a video which demonstrates how to connect the MIDI adapter cable, see the "MIDI Cable Installation Video" section which follows.

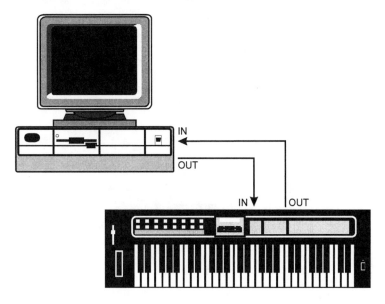

Typical MIDI setup with a musical keyboard

MIDI Cable Installation Video

We've included a video which demonstrates how to connect a MIDI cable. This video is in MediaCheck.™

To view the video:

1. Put the Teach Me Piano disc in the CD-ROM drive.
2. In the Voyetra Teach Me Piano program group, click the icon for MediaCheck.
3. In MediaCheck, click Setup Tips at the bottom left of the screen.
4. When asked if you want to view instructions on setting up your external keyboard, click Yes.
5. Sit back and watch the video!

Switching Applications

If you want to switch from Teach Me Piano to another Windows application, you can do so by using the standard Windows shortcut keys:

KEYSTROKE   **WHAT IT DOES**

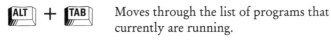 Moves through the list of programs that currently are running.

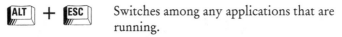 Switches among any applications that are running.

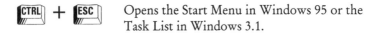 Opens the Start Menu in Windows 95 or the Task List in Windows 3.1.

 "Multitasking" — running several applications at the same time — can slow down performance and cause problems. To free up system resources and avoid potential problems, we recommend you close down any other applications before running Teach Me Piano.

Chapter 3

Quick Overview

Teach Me Piano is composed of four modules:

- **Keyboard Lessons** is an in-depth piano course taught by a professional music teacher.

- **Songbook** stores the songs that come with the program and lets you listen to them, play them with accompaniment, import your own MIDI files and print them.

- **Musician's Reference** is a guide to the basics of musical notation.

- **MediaCheck™** lets you test and troubleshoot the multimedia devices on your computer.

There's also an:

- **Online Catalog** to learn about Voyetra's other exciting music software products.

 To interrupt the Introduction and go directly to the Piano Room, click ESC while the Voyetra Logo Introduction is playing.

The Piano Room

The Piano Room is the opening screen in Teach Me Piano. From this screen, you can access all of the parts of the program.

Click to open the **Songbook**.

Click to start **MediaCheck**.

Click to view the **Musician's Reference**.

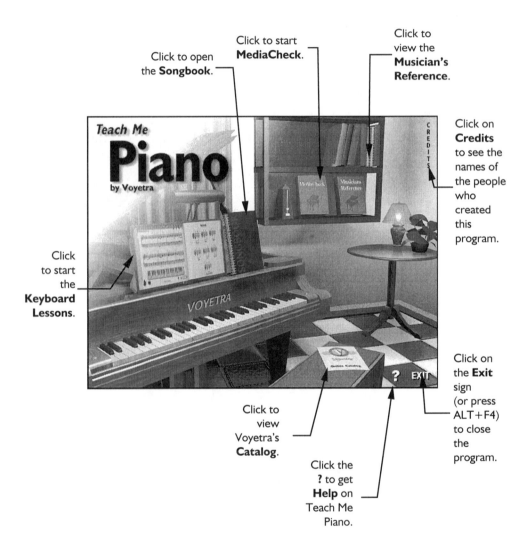

Click on **Credits** to see the names of the people who created this program.

Click to start the **Keyboard Lessons**.

Click on the **Exit** sign (or press ALT+F4) to close the program.

Click to view Voyetra's **Catalog**.

Click the **?** to get **Help** on Teach Me Piano.

The Pop-Up Menu

Clicking the right mouse button in the Piano Room displays a pop-up menu.

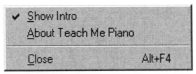

The right-click pop-up menu

From this menu, you can:

- **Toggle the Voyetra Introduction on or off.**

    - A check mark next to "Show Intro" indicates that the Introduction will play when the program starts up. (No check mark indicates that the Introduction will not play when the program starts.)

    - "On" is the default setting for the Introduction (check mark displayed).

- **View "About" information** — including version number, product ID number, the name of the person to whom the software is licensed and copyright date.

- **Close the program** without the final musical "goodbye."

 You will need the Product ID number if you phone for Technical Support. This number can be found in the "About" box.

Keyboard Shortcut Keys

Here's a list of keyboard shortcut keys that make the Keyboard Lessons and the Songbook easier to use:

KEYSTROKE   FUNCTION

 Stops/Plays media elements — as an alternative to clicking on the Clapboard (slate).

 Returns to Keyboard Lessons' Contents screen.

 Pages forward within the lesson.

 Pages backward within the lesson.

 Prints the Performance and Progress screens.

 Goes back to the previous manuscript page (of music).

 Goes forward to the next manuscript page (of music).

 Use instead of clicking on "Do It."

 Use instead of clicking on "See It."

Chapter 4

Musician's Reference

With easy-to-understand definitions, diagrams and illustrations the Musician's Reference is a handy guide when learning about musical notation.

There are eight main sections in the Musician's Reference:

- The Staff
- Pitches and Clefs
- Rhythms
- Barlines, Measures and Time Signatures
- Key Signatures
- Dynamics
- Tempo
- Lyrics

When you wish to learn more about a particular topic, just click the green, underlined words. These links to other topics help tie-in related concepts and make it easy to navigate through the screens in the Musician's Reference.

 To load the Musician's Reference, click the Musician's Reference book on the bookshelf in the Piano Room.

Getting Around

To move from one topic to another:

- Click the green, underlined words to "jump" to a definition of the word you clicked on.

- To return to the definition you previously jumped from, click the Back button.

Click the **Search** button to locate a topic.

Click the **Back** button to return to the previous topic.

Click the **Print** button to print the current page.

Click the **Contents** button to return to the Musician's Reference Main Screen.

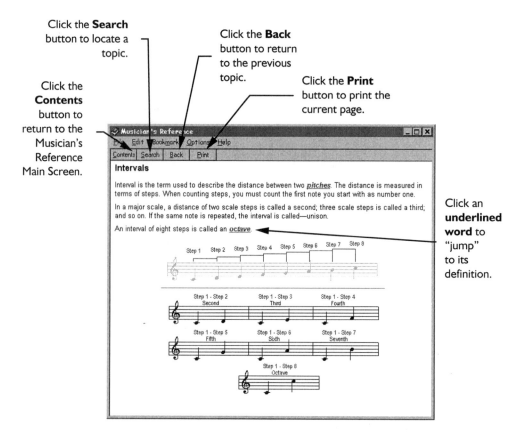

Click an **underlined word** to "jump" to its definition.

Chapter 5

Keyboard Lessons

In Keyboard Lessons, a professional music teacher introduces you to basic music notation, theory and playing technique through a series of video clips, exercises and songs. With more than 150 lessons and over 100 exercises, there is a full course of study. Beginners can learn basic techniques while intermediate players can reinforce their musical skills. When you complete the entire program, you will have learned to play more than 75 well-known songs!

The interactive computer training system provides analysis and feedback in each lesson and tracks your progress. This helps you focus on the areas in which you need more practice.

After you have learned a song, click on Performance to play it with background accompaniment. At the end of the performance, you'll be rewarded with a favorable round of applause from the virtual audience!

 To load Keyboard Lessons, click the sheet music on the piano's music stand in the Piano Room.

The Lessons

Keyboard Lessons is designed so that you can study at your own pace — as quickly or slowly as you would like.

You are probably very eager to get started — and that is good — but we recommend that you pace yourself. Take your time. Don't try to complete the lessons in a rush.

All of the Lessons are designed to build on each other, so it is important that you fully understand the concepts and techniques in one Lesson before you move on to the next.

 You'll learn more if you spend 16 half-hour sessions over several weeks with Keyboard Lessons than if you work at the program for a single, 8-hour marathon session.

Preparing to Play

One of the most important factors in playing piano is how you sit at the keyboard. You should not have to strain to read the music.

Sit on a comfortable chair and place your hands on the piano keyboard. Keep both feet on the floor — no dangling feet. For younger students, place a stool or a stack of phone books under their feet so they, too, can sit properly.

When you place your hands down, the keyboard should be slightly lower than your elbows. This gives you a natural position.

Close your hands into fists (not too tightly) and place them on the keyboard. Make sure your wrists are comfortable and not hanging too low. Slowly open your hands until they have a natural shape. Watch that your thumbs do not fall off the keyboard. This is good hand positioning at the piano keyboard.

Computer Keyboard/Musical Keyboard Setup

A comfortable arrangement of the monitor, computer
and musical keyboard is important!

When using Teach Me Piano, it is important to have the computer keyboard, mouse and monitor — as well as the musical keyboard — arranged comfortably.

Place yourself in the center of the piano keyboard by locating Middle C. Remember that you are going to need the mouse and computer keyboard alongside the piano keyboard, so place them in a location that's comfortable to reach.

You should be able to see the monitor easily, without straining your eyes and/or your neck. Remember, you should be reading the monitor and not looking down at your fingers on the piano keyboard. This helps build confidence when playing the musical keyboard.

Computer music setups will vary. Use your best judgment when arranging your system — and remember that you should always be comfortable and never strain.

Enter and Sign In, Please

Keyboard Lessons can keep track of many users' progress. This means that all of the members of your family can learn to play — at their own pace — and Teach Me Piano will keep track of them individually.

When you open Keyboard Lessons, you are presented with the Student Registration screen. If you are a new student, you need to enter your name and let Teach Me Piano know what level student you are.

 The three levels — Beginner, Intermediate and Advanced — all contain the same songs. The difference between the levels is how you are scored during the evaluations. If you select a higher level, the program will be more exacting when evaluating your playing.

To sign in as a new user:

1. Click New on the Student Registration screen to display the "Enter new user name" dialog box.

2. Type in your name and click the appropriate skill level — Beginner, Intermediate or Advanced.

3. Click OK to return to the Student Registration screen.

"Enter new user name" dialog box

 If you are a Discovering Keyboards user who clicked "Yes" during installation to transfer your user information into Teach Me Piano, your name and level will already, automatically have been recorded!

To run Keyboard Lessons after you've signed in:

Once you have entered your name as a new user, your name will appear in the Student Registration dialog box.

1. Click your name to select it.
2. Click OK. Your name will appear as "Current Student" on the front of the piano.

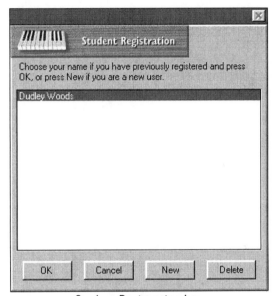

Student Registration box

 It is important to always sign in under the same user name. This way, when you return to Keyboard Lessons, the program can pick up where you left off the last time and keep track of your progress.

Keyboard Lessons' Contents Screen

The contents of the Keyboard Lessons are displayed in the full view of the Keyboard Lessons Training Handbook, as shown below.

Keyboard Lessons is divided into six **Sections**. When you click on a Section, the Section name changes from black to blue to show it has been selected.

Each **Section** is divided into five **Chapters**, each with a series of **Lessons**.

Click **Songbook** to go to the Songbook.

The **name** of the student currently using the program displays here.

Click the **magnifying glass** to view the list of Lessons in a specific Chapter.

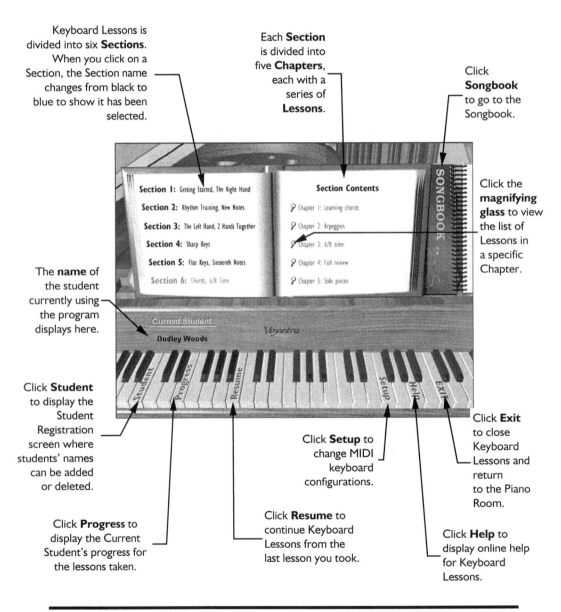

Click **Student** to display the Student Registration screen where students' names can be added or deleted.

Click **Progress** to display the Current Student's progress for the lessons taken.

Click **Resume** to continue Keyboard Lessons from the last lesson you took.

Click **Setup** to change MIDI keyboard configurations.

Click **Help** to display online help for Keyboard Lessons.

Click **Exit** to close Keyboard Lessons and return to the Piano Room.

Overview of the Sections

Keyboard Lessons is divided into six main Sections. Each section contains five chapters, the chapters contain the individual lessons.

 For a detailed list of the lessons, refer to the Appendix at the back of this book.

Section 1

The basic elements of Keyboard Lessons are described in Section 1, with tutorials to help you navigate quickly and easily through the Lessons.

Section 1 guides you through some of the basic elements of piano performance. To make things easier, you'll begin with playing by ear. Just watch and listen closely and you'll be amazed at how quickly you start playing the piano keyboard.

The staff and the names of the notes — both on the piano keyboard and the grand staff — are introduced. Counting basic rhythms as well as the half notes and quarter notes are also introduced here. By the end of the chapter, you'll begin playing Beethoven's Ode to Joy!

As the section continues, there are exercises and new songs to reinforce the basic structure of music. You'll learn the C scale in Chapter 3 and intervals in Chapter 4. You'll be impressed with all of the new songs you soon will be playing.

Section 2

Section 2 starts off with rhythm. It explores grouping beats and eighth notes, as well as the different time signatures and rests.

Chapter 3 introduces sharps and flats; Chapter 4 moves along to octaves with exercises to reinforce them and upbeats and downbeats.

By Chapter 5 dotted-half and dotted-quarter notes are introduced.

Section 3

In Section 3, you'll learn about the bass clef and the left hand and play a few more exercises. You'll explore the grand staff and more of the C scale — including contrary and parallel motion. Throughout the rest of this section there are finger workouts, Ode to Joy using both hands, and many new songs to learn.

Section 4

Key signatures are introduced in Section 4, beginning with the sharp keys of G Major, D Major and A Major. There are exercises to help get you quickly adjusted to each key, as well as songs to help reinforce your playing in these new keys.

In Chapter 4, there are songs that contain tied notes, and in Chapter 5, you'll begin playing with both hands together.

Section 5

After learning about sharp keys in Section 4, you'll move on to flat keys in Section 5. These include the keys of F Major and B-flat Major.

More focus is brought to rhythm, with the attention on sixteenth notes in Chapter 3. Chapter 4 expands on this with exercises, and in Chapter 5, there are many new pieces to play including Danse Macabre.

Section 6

In Section 6, you begin playing block chords in both the left and right hands and then move on to incorporating the chords into songs. The next step is arpeggios, where you open the chords by playing the individual notes within them. Greensleeves, a fun song to learn, is included in this section, and the newly-learned techniques make it even easier to play.

In Chapter 3, 6/8 time is introduced and by end of the section there are exciting songs to play including the Marionette March, Waltz in C, the Can-Can and many others.

As a New User

As a new student in Keyboard Lessons, you will want to begin at the beginning — Section 1, Chapter 1, Lesson 1. Click the magnifying glass to display the Table of Contents screen which lists the lessons.

You can go to any Lesson at any time. If you feel you need to review a Chapter, just click on its name.

Click a lesson name to select (highlight) it.

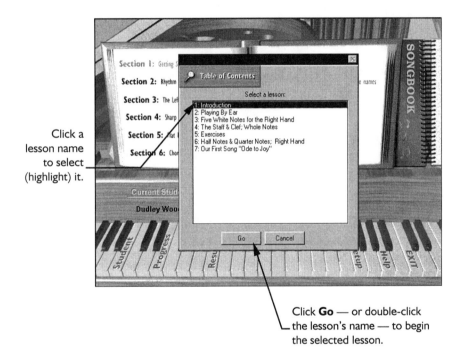

Click **Go** — or double-click the lesson's name — to begin the selected lesson.

Although the beginning lessons may seem easy at first — especially if you've had some prior musical training — it is important to go through the lessons in order, since new skills are built from lesson to lesson.

Keyboard Shortcut Keys

A listing of Keyboard Shortcut Keys can be found in the "Quick Overview" chapter.

Screens in Keyboard Lessons

There are several different kinds of screens in Keyboard Lessons.

Contents Screen	Is the main screen in Teach Me Piano. This screen displays the Keyboard Lessons Training Handbook with Section Contents for the lessons.
Information Screen	Displays the Lesson's content, including text, graphics, videos and animations.
Video Screen	Is located within the Information screen. It displays video examples and tutorials to help guide you through the lessons.
Trainer Screen	Contains the Rhythm, Pitch, Rhythm & Pitch Trainers as well as the Perform, Do It, Range and See It icons in the toolbar at the top of the screen.
Evaluation Screen	Is only displayed after training with Rhythm & Pitch. This screen shows how well you did when practicing and breaks down the evaluation into specific areas to help you improve your playing.
Performance Screen	Displays "sheet music" so you can play along with a back-up band.
Chapter Review Screen	Displays at the end of each chapter. From this screen you can view a progress report or continue on to the next chapter.
Progress Screen	This screen shows how well you did in the chapters of that particular section. It is accessed either from the Contents screen or a Chapter Review screen.

The Information Screen

The Information Screen displays the Lesson's content. It includes text, graphics, animations, videos and examples.

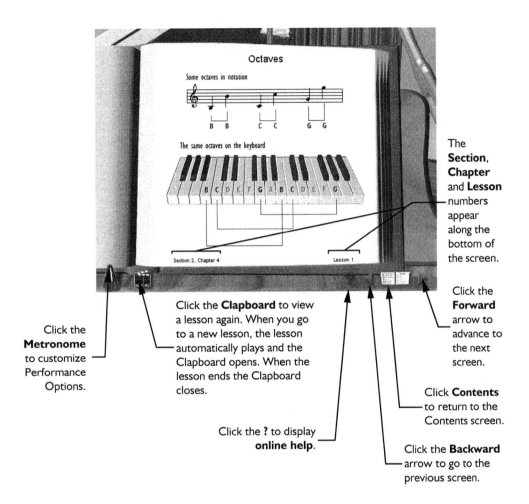

The **Section**, **Chapter** and **Lesson** numbers appear along the bottom of the screen.

Click the **Forward** arrow to advance to the next screen.

Click the **Metronome** to customize Performance Options.

Click the **Clapboard** to view a lesson again. When you go to a new lesson, the lesson automatically plays and the Clapboard opens. When the lesson ends the Clapboard closes.

Click **Contents** to return to the Contents screen.

Click the **?** to display **online help**.

Click the **Backward** arrow to go to the previous screen.

Adjusting the Volume in Keyboard Lessons

If you find the volume too loud or too soft in Keyboard Lessons, use the Performance Options dialog box — click on the Metronome — to adjust it.

The Video Screen

The Video Screen contains video examples and tutorials to help guide you through the lessons.

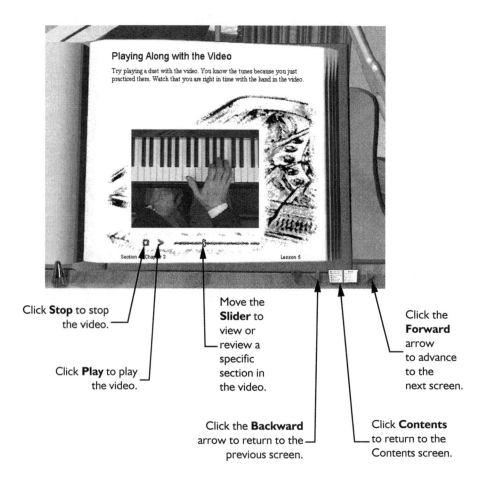

Click **Stop** to stop the video.

Click **Play** to play the video.

Move the **Slider** to view or review a specific section in the video.

Click the **Backward** arrow to return to the previous screen.

Click the **Forward** arrow to advance to the next screen.

Click **Contents** to return to the Contents screen.

So that you'll have time to "digest" what you have learned, the Lessons do not advance automatically. After a presentation ends — when you are ready to continue on — click the Forward arrow to advance to the next Lesson.

The Trainer Screen

The Enhanced Toolbar along the top of the screen contains the Rhythm, Pitch, Rhythm & Pitch Trainers and the Perform, Do It, Range and See It icons. Not all pieces in Lessons contain both the left and right hands. In such cases, sections of the Toolbar are not available.

Click **Perform** to display the Performance screen.

Click **Do It** to begin an exercise. Click Do It again to stop the exercise.

Rhythm & Pitch sets the hand(s) for practicing both rhythm and pitch — left, right or both.

Range sets which measures you want to practice.

Pitch Trainer sets the hand(s) for practicing pitch — left, right or both.

Click **See It** to hear the piece performed for you. Click again to stop the performance.

Rhythm Trainer sets the hand(s) for practicing rhythm — left, right or both.

Click the **Page Forward** arrow to move ahead a page in the musical score.

Click the **Page Back** arrow to go back a page. Don't mix up these arrows with the Forward and Backward arrows at the bottom of the screen which move you from screen to screen.

Click the **Metronome** to open the Performance Options dialog box.

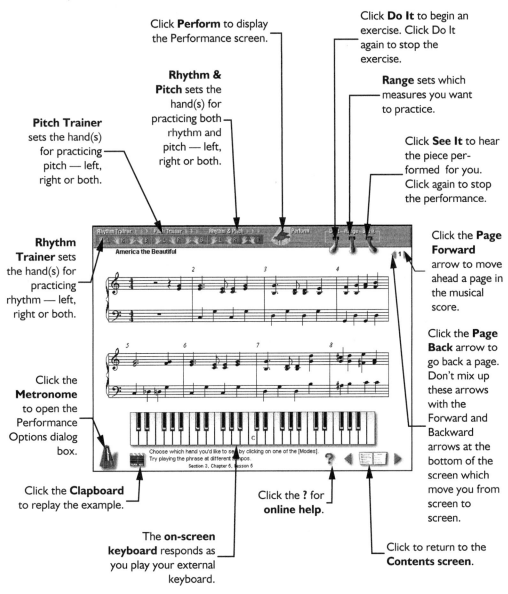

Click the **Clapboard** to replay the example.

Click the **?** for **online help**.

The **on-screen keyboard** responds as you play your external keyboard.

Click to return to the **Contents screen**.

Using the Trainer Screen

From the Trainer screen, you can practice rhythm, pitch or rhythm and pitch together, with just the left or right hand or with both hands. Click the icons on the Enhanced Toolbar to make your choices.

The Enhanced Toolbar on the Trainer Screen

 If you wish to hear the rhythm or pitch performed for you, click "See It" or press CTRL + Enter.

Practicing Rhythm — Getting the Beats Right

Practicing rhythm helps you gain a better understanding of meter and improves your counting. It is one of the most difficult components of music to play correctly. You may find that rhythm does not come easily — but don't get discouraged. If you find you are having a problem, try slowing down the tempo. As you improve, increase the tempo (see Lesson Tempo in the Performance Options dialog box).

Practicing Pitch — Getting the Notes Right

The more you practice playing pitches, the better your note-reading skills will become. The Enhanced Toolbar makes it easy to practice pitch.

Fingering is very important when practicing pitches. Be sure to play each note using the finger numbers indicated on the musical score. Go slowly, there is no time limit. Remember to keep your wrists parallel with your keyboard; do not let your wrists fall below the keyboard you are playing.

NOTE If you are unsure about hand position, place a quarter on the back of each hand. As you play, don't let the quarter fall off. Keep your wrists straight and your hands parallel with the keyboard. Once you can play without the quarters falling off your hands, take them off and remember how your arms, wrists and hands felt in the proper position.

Practicing Rhythm & Pitch — Getting Beats and Notes Right

Rhythm and pitch together make the personality of a tune — you can't have one without the other! Use the Enhanced Toolbar to practice rhythm and pitch together.

To practice rhythm, pitch, or rhythm & pitch:

1. On the Enhanced Toolbar under Rhythm Trainer , Pitch Trainer or Rhythm & Pitch, click the icon for the hand(s) you would like to practice.

2. Click Do It or press Enter.

3. **FOR RHYTHM:** After the metronome gives a count-in measure (the number of count-in measures can be adjusted in the Performance Options dialog box), begin playing the correct rhythm on your MIDI keyboard as the pointer moves over each note. You can use any key on the MIDI keyboard to play the rhythm.

    FOR PITCH: Play the key on your MIDI keyboard which corresponds with the note the pointer is positioned over. When you press the correct key, the pointer advances to the next note. If you press a wrong key, a "honk" sounds and the pointer does not advance until you play the note correctly.

4. When you have finished practicing, an evaluation of your performance displays at the bottom of the screen.

NOTE When Keyboard Lessons is running, you can play your MIDI keyboard at any time. If you want to practice a piece without an evaluation, just start playing. If the piece is more than one page, click the Page Forward or Page Back arrows at the top of the screen to turn the pages.

The Performance Screen

When you feel confident with a piece you have been working on, it's time to perform it. On the Performance screen, .sheet music is displayed on screen as you play along with a background ensemble.

To perform a piece:

1. Click Perform to display the Performance screen.
2. When you are ready to begin, click Do It. Click again to stop.
3. If you want to hear the piece performed for you, click See It. Click again to stop.
4. When you are finished, click Trainer to return to the Practice Screen.

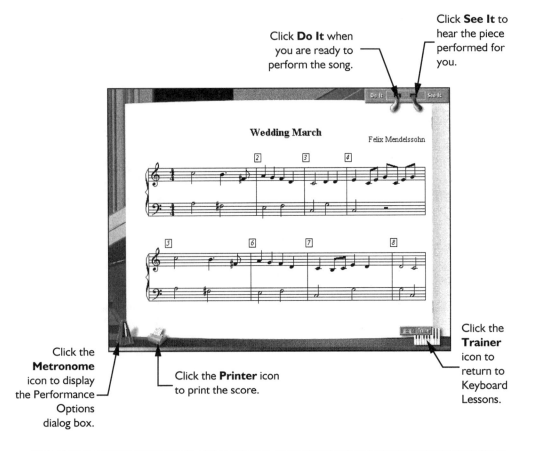

Click **Do It** when you are ready to perform the song.

Click **See It** to hear the piece performed for you.

Click the **Metronome** icon to display the Performance Options dialog box.

Click the **Printer** icon to print the score.

Click the **Trainer** icon to return to Keyboard Lessons.

Performance Options

Clicking on the metronome displays the Performance Options dialog box. Performance Options can be changed at any time in Keyboard Lesson.

Solo raises and lowers the volume for the main instrument.

Solo Instrument changes the main instrument you are using.

Page Turn Anticipation selects the number of sixteenth notes that are counted before turning the page.

Finger numbers displays the finger numbers. This feature works only with songs that came with Teach Me Piano.

Note names displays the names of the notes. This option works with all pieces — including any MIDI files you import.

Accomp. raises and lowers the volume for the accompaniment.

Narration raises and lowers the volume for the audio narrations.

Metronome Lead-in selects the number of measures for count-in, before you begin playing.

Lesson Tempo adjusts the tempo for the pieces, both for practicing and performance.

Perform video toggles on/off the introduction to the Performance screen.

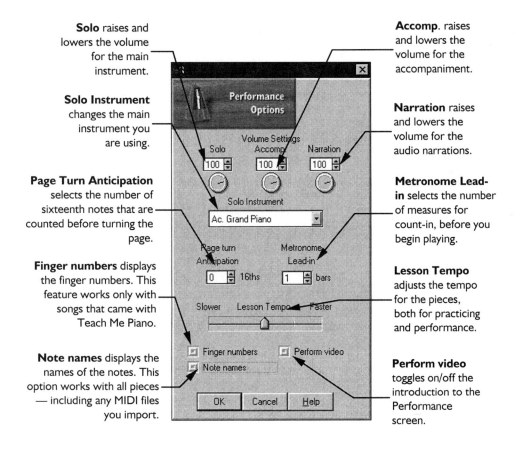

 "Note names" works on the all files the came with Teach Me Piano. For it to work properly with imported MIDI files, the files need to be quantized first. Refer to your sequencer's manual on how to quantize MIDI files.

Evaluation Screen

The Evaluation screen is only displayed after training with Rhythm & Pitch. This screen shows how well you did when practicing. It breaks down the evaluation into specific areas to help you improve your playing.

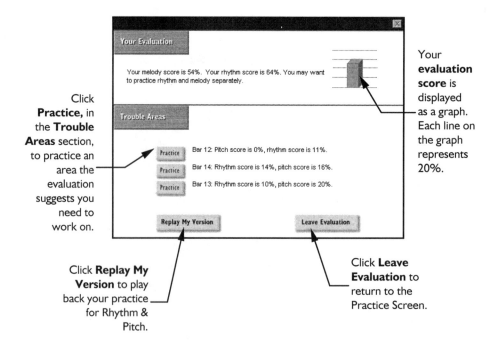

Your **evaluation score** is displayed as a graph. Each line on the graph represents 20%.

Click **Practice,** in the **Trouble Areas** section, to practice an area the evaluation suggests you need to work on.

Click **Replay My Version** to play back your practice for Rhythm & Pitch.

Click **Leave Evaluation** to return to the Practice Screen.

The "Trouble Areas" which you need to practice are listed from the most mistakes to the least mistakes. If you played the piece well, the Trouble Areas section will not display.

To practice an area from the Evaluation Screen:

1. Click Practice to return to the Practice screen. Notice that both the practice area and the Range button are selected.

2. Press Enter or click Do It for a count-in.

3. Begin playing. When you are done, you are returned to the Evaluation Screen where the section you just played will be evaluated.

4. If you wish to practice another section, click Practice again. Remember: practice makes perfect!

When you click on a practice button in the evaluation, you are returned to the Trainer screen, with the **Range pedal** selected.

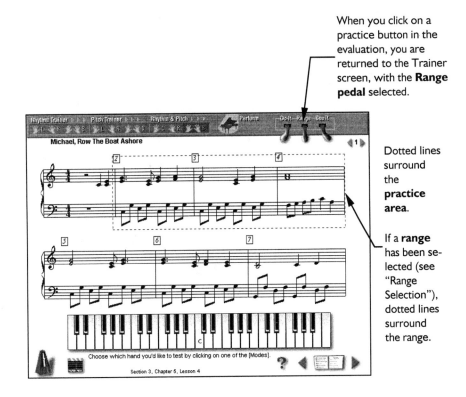

Dotted lines surround the **practice area**.

If a **range** has been selected (see "Range Selection"), dotted lines surround the range.

 When you are practicing a section from the Evaluation Screen, you cannot change the Range.

Range Selection

Sometimes, a section of a piece may be difficult to master. The Range button lets you practice that section as many times as you'd like.

Click the **icons for the hand(s)** you would like to practice in Rhythm, Pitch, or Rhythm & Pitch.

Click the **Range** pedal to select a range to practice.

The Enhanced Toolbar on the Trainer Screen

Click **Entire Piece** to practice the entire song.

Click **Practice Range** to set a range of measures to practice.

Click **OK** to return to the Trainer screen where the measure(s) you chose to practice appear surrounded by dotted lines.

The **From** box indicates the first measure in the range you wish to practice.

The **Thru** box indicates the last measure in the range you wish to practice.

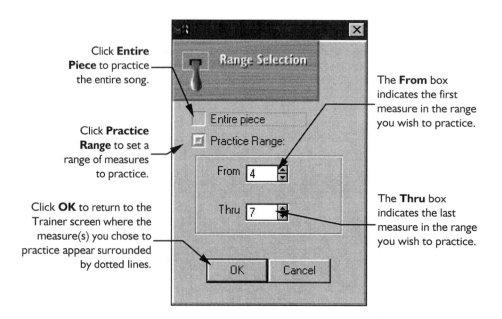

If you wish to practice only one measure, enter the measure number in both the From and Thru boxes.

- To set the range for the entire piece, click Entire Piece. The From and Thru boxes will no longer be available.

Chapter Review Screen

At the end of each chapter, the Chapter Review screen displays. From here, you can see a Progress Report on how you've done so far or continue on to the next Chapter.

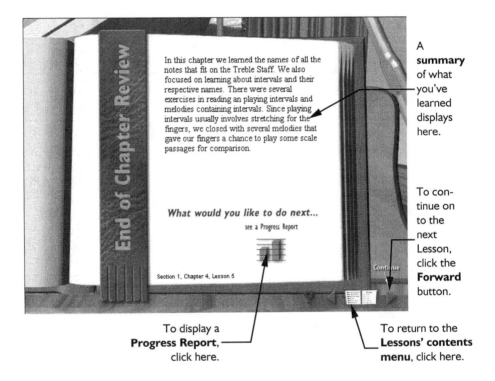

A **summary** of what you've learned displays here.

In this chapter we learned the names of all the notes that fit on the Treble Staff. We also focused on learning about intervals and their respective names. There were several exercises in reading an playing intervals and melodies containing intervals. Since playing intervals usually involves stretching for the fingers, we closed with several melodies that gave our fingers a chance to play some scale passages for comparison.

What would you like to do next...

see a Progress Report

Section 1, Chapter 4, Lesson 5

Continue

To continue on to the next Lesson, click the **Forward** button.

To display a **Progress Report**, click here.

To return to the **Lessons' contents menu**, click here.

Self-Paced Learning

As you study the lessons, remember that they are self-paced — you can move along as quickly or slowly as you'd like. Take your time and don't rush. Remember, practice makes perfect!

 You can go to any Lesson at any time. If you feel you need to review a specific lesson, just click on its name.

Progress Screen

the Progress screen can be accessed from any Chapter Review screen or from the Contents screen. This screen shows how well you did in each Chapter of that particular Section.

The **current Student's name** is displayed here.

The name of the **Section** that has been selected appears in white print.

To see the **Progress for another Section**, click on the appropriate button.

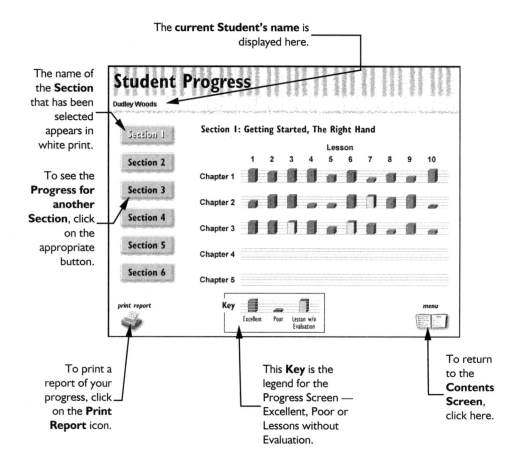

To print a report of your progress, click on the **Print Report** icon.

This **Key** is the legend for the Progress Screen — Excellent, Poor or Lessons without Evaluation.

To return to the **Contents Screen**, click here.

 If you go to the Progress Screen from Keyboard Lessons, the icon reads "Return to Review." If you go from the Contents Screen. the icon reads "Menu." Click either one to return the appropriate screen.

Changing the Setup in the Keyboard Lessons

When you first install Teach Me Piano, you are prompted to set up your MIDI configurations. Therefore, it is unlikely that you will need to open the Setup dialog box while going through the Lessons. However, if your MIDI keyboard is not responding when using Keyboard Lessons, check to make sure the settings in the Setup box are correct.

In the **MIDI Input Device** box, choose the MIDI port you want to receive MIDI information from. This can be your sound card or a MIDI interface. This box only displays available MIDI ports.

When checked, **MIDI Thru** is turned On, it allows MIDI data to be echoed to the MIDI Out port. On is the default setting for this option. If you are using a keyboard that plays through your sound card, you'll hear the sound through your computer's speakers or headphones only when MIDI Thru is set to On.

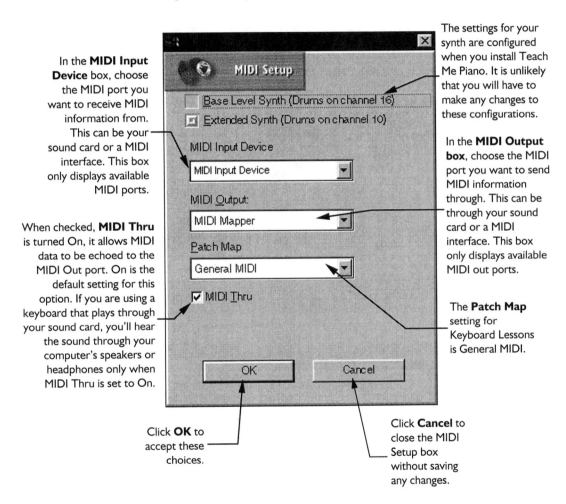

The settings for your synth are configured when you install Teach Me Piano. It is unlikely that you will have to make any changes to these configurations.

In the **MIDI Output** box, choose the MIDI port you want to send MIDI information through. This can be through your sound card or a MIDI interface. This box only displays available MIDI out ports.

The **Patch Map** setting for Keyboard Lessons is General MIDI.

Click **OK** to accept these choices.

Click **Cancel** to close the MIDI Setup box without saving any changes.

Base and Extended Level Synths

Base and Extended Level synth determine how MIDI data is sent through your sound card.

- A Base Level Synth uses only Channels 13 through 16, where Channel 16 is the reserved for percussion.

- An Extended Level Synth uses only Channels 1 through 10, where Channel 10 is reserved for percussion.

 It is unlikely that you will have to make any changes to these configurations. For additional information, refer to the hardware manual for your sound card.

Using Note Names and Finger Numbers

You will find that as the complexity of the music increases, there will be a greater number of note names and finger numbers above and below the staff; this can make reading the music more cumbersome. As the lessons become more difficult — and your skills increase — there should no longer be a need to have the Note Names option enabled all the time. Disabling this option will reduce the amount of text on the screen.

The Finger Numbers option also can be disabled to help "clean up" the screen for greater clarity when reading the notes. Should you require assistance with the proper fingering for a piece, you can always enable Finger Numbers at any time.

Chapter 6

Songbook

The Songbook in Teach Me Piano includes the more than 75 songs — classics, folk tunes, holiday and patriotic songs, and more. You also can import your own MIDI song files and print them out — complete with note names — on your computer's printer.

There are four "Tabs" along the right edge of the Songbook. These help you organize and locate the songs by Title, Style, Composer and Level of Difficulty.

From the Songbook, you can access either the Trainer screen where you can practice the selected song, or the Performance screen where you can play the songs with background accompaniment. If you chose the Performance Screen, when you finish playing, the audience will reward you with a warm round of applause!

 To load the Songbook, click the green Songbook on the piano's music stand in the Piano Room. You also can load the Songbook from Keyboard Lessons' Contents Screen.

Songbook Screen

Click the **Trainer** icon to practice the selected song.

Click the **Piano** icon to perform a song in the Songbook with background accompaniment.

Click **Import MIDI** to import your own songs into the Songbook.

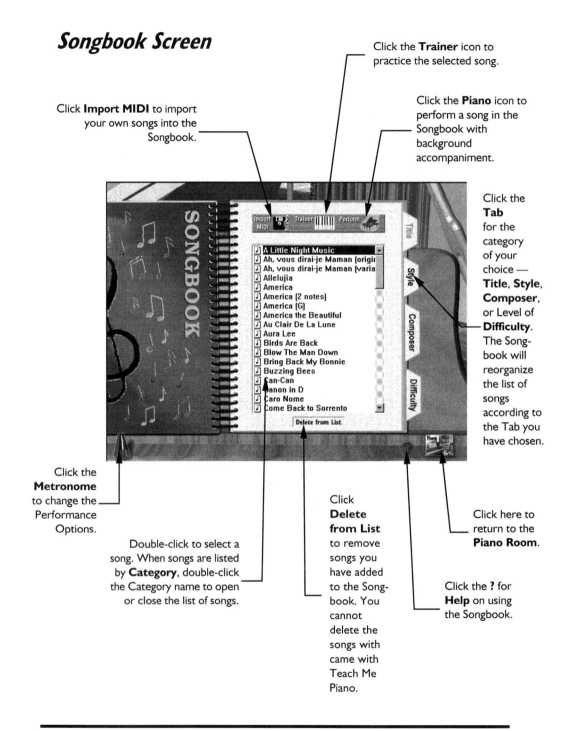

Click the **Tab** for the category of your choice — **Title**, **Style**, **Composer**, or Level of **Difficulty**. The Songbook will reorganize the list of songs according to the Tab you have chosen.

A Little Night Music
Ah, vous dirai-je Maman (origii
Ah, vous dirai-je Maman (varia
Allelujia
America
America (2 notes)
America [G]
America the Beautiful
Au Clair De La Lune
Aura Lee
Birds Are Back
Blow The Man Down
Bring Back My Bonnie
Buzzing Bees
Can-Can
Canon in D
Caro Nome
Come Back to Sorrento

Delete from List

Click the **Metronome** to change the Performance Options.

Double-click to select a song. When songs are listed by **Category**, double-click the Category name to open or close the list of songs.

Click **Delete from List** to remove songs you have added to the Songbook. You cannot delete the songs with came with Teach Me Piano.

Click here to return to the **Piano Room**.

Click the **?** for **Help** on using the Songbook.

Organizing Songs in the Songbook

The Songbook resembles a real book — with Tabs for different sections. The songs in the Songbook can be arranged in four different ways — by Title, Style, Composer or Level of Difficulty.

Title   Lists the songs in alphabetical order, by title.

Style   Organizes the songs according to different styles: Classical, Folk, Holiday, Patriotic, Ragtime, and Traditional.

Composer   Finds a song by a particular composer. When there is no known composer, the songs are listed by category such as American Folk Tune, French Carol, French Folk Tune, German Folk Tune, etc.

Difficulty   Arranges the songs by difficulty — with the easiest listed first, the most difficult last. The order of songs in this Tab follows the order in which the songs are presented in the Keyboard Lessons.

 In the Songbook, the Title and Difficulty sections list each song individually. The Style and Composer sections have categories where groups of individual songs are located.

In the Composer section, if the composer is anonymous, the song will be listed under the geographical area from which it originated.

Keyboard Shortcut Keys

There are several keyboard shortcut keys that make the Songbook and Keyboard Lessons easier to use. A listing of these can be found in the "Quick Overview" chapter.

If you are a Discovering Keyboards user who clicked "Yes" during installation to transfer your user information into Teach Me Piano, any songs which you imported into the Songbook in Discovering Keyboards will automatically have been brought over to the Teach Me Piano Songbook.

Importing a Song

The songs you can perform are not limited to those which came with Teach Me Piano. If you have songs in MIDI format, you can add them to the Songbook and then print them out, complete with note names.

To import a song:

1. Click the Import MIDI button at the top of the screen.
2. Using the Open dialog box, locate the file you want to import.
3. Double-click the desired file name to display the Import MIDI File dialog box.
4. After entering the appropriate information, click OK to add your song to the Songbook.

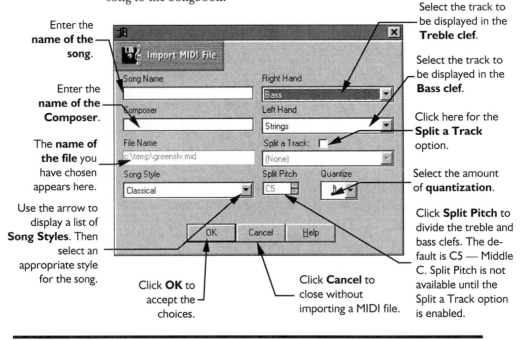

Enter the **name of the song**.

Enter the **name of the Composer**.

The **name of the file** you have chosen appears here.

Use the arrow to display a list of **Song Styles**. Then select an appropriate style for the song.

Click **OK** to accept the choices.

Select the track to be displayed in the **Treble clef**.

Select the track to be displayed in the **Bass clef**.

Click here for the **Split a Track** option.

Select the amount of **quantization**.

Click **Split Pitch** to divide the treble and bass clefs. The default is C5 — Middle C. Split Pitch is not available until the Split a Track option is enabled.

Click **Cancel** to close without importing a MIDI file.

When Importing Files

- The Import dialog box allows you to import both .MID and .ORC files. .ORC files are Voyetra's proprietary sequencer files which can be produced with Voyetra's MIDI Orchestrator Plus™ and Digital Orchestrator Plus.™

- Some .ORC files may contain digital audio. If you import a file with digital audio, the digital audio tracks will be ignored when importing, and these tracks will be deleted when the file is saved in Teach Me Piano.

- Imported files are saved on your hard drive in the \voyetra\teachme directory. These files are saved with the .ORC extension.

- The Songbook only displays notation in the Grand Staff. You can import a song with more than two tracks, but only two tracks will be displayed. However, you will hear the other tracks playing. This can be useful when you want to learn a part in a song you've imported. Then, when you feel confident with it, click Do It in the Performance Screen and you can perform the song with the other tracks in the MIDI file.

- If you import a file that contains only one track, it defaults to the treble clef — and only the treble clef displays. If you change the track to display in the bass clef, the entire grand staff displays.

Deleting a Song from the Songbook

Only songs that have been imported can be deleted from the Songbook. All the imported songs have the word "Import" next to them in parentheses.

To delete a song from the Songbook:

1. Click on the Song Name you wish to delete.
2. Click the Delete from List box at the bottom of the screen. You are prompted with a dialog box that asks if you are sure you wish to delete the file.
3. Click Yes to delete the file.

Split a Track Option

Many times, a MIDI file is recorded onto a single track. This makes it difficult to display as piano notation. If you wish to see a single track notated in the grand staff, use the Split a Track option.

To use the Split a Track option:

Be sure the Import MIDI file box is already open and you have entered the song's name and composer, set the song style and the level of quantization.

1. Click the Split a Track check box. A check mark appears, the Right Hand and Left Hand boxes dim, and the Split Pitch box is enabled.
2. In the Split a Track box, select the track to be notated.
3. In the Split Pitch spin box, select the pitch that will divide the treble and bass clefs. The default is C5 (middle C).
4. When you are satisfied with your choices, click OK.

 The Quantize feature breaks the notes into the smallest division selected. You can choose a quantization range from whole notes to sixty-fourth notes. If you choose quarter notes, you will only see whole notes, half notes, and quarter notes. The most common choice is sixteenth notes. Quantize only affects the notation and how it displays, it will not alter the MIDI file itself.

Performance Screen

You can access the Performance screen both from Keyboard Lessons and from the Songbook. On this screen, sheet music is displayed as you play along with a background ensemble. When you are finished playing, you are rewarded with a warm round of applause from the "audience."

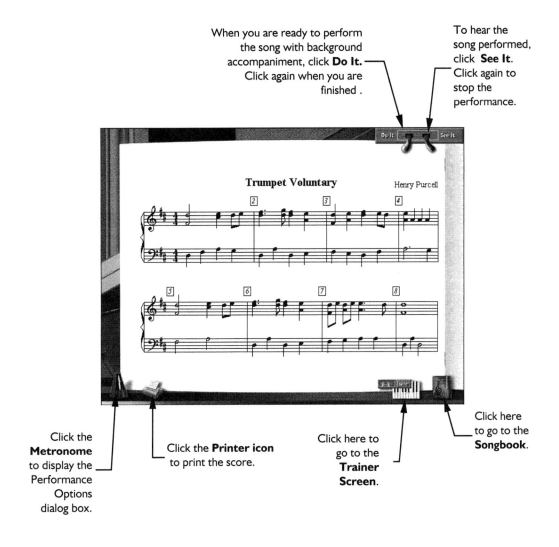

When you are ready to perform the song with background accompaniment, click **Do It.** Click again when you are finished .

To hear the song performed, click **See It**. Click again to stop the performance.

Click the **Metronome** to display the Performance Options dialog box.

Click the **Printer icon** to print the score.

Click here to go to the **Trainer Screen**.

Click here to go to the **Songbook**.

From the Performance Screen you can:

- Go to the Songbook, by clicking its icon, to choose another song to perform.

- Go to the Trainer Screen, by clicking its icon, to practice the currently loaded song.

- Turn off the Performance Introduction video by clicking Perform Video located in the Performance Options box. (Click the metronome at the bottom left of the screen to display this dialog box.)

- Access any options in the Performance Options box.

- Play your imported MIDI files in the Performance screen. Even though you see only the notation for the tracks you specified in the Import dialog box, you will head the entire MIDI file, including all of its tracks.

Printing a Song

Any song in the Songbook can be printed — even MIDI files you have imported into the Songbook.

To print a song:

1. Double-click on the song's name to display the Performance Screen.

2. Click the printer icon at the bottom of the screen to display a standard Windows Print dialog box.

If you would like to see note names and finger numbers on the print out, click the Performance Options icon and select "Finger Numbers" and/or "Note Names." However, finger numbers cannot be printed for songs that have been imported . For imported songs, Teach Me Piano can only print note names.

Chapter 7

MediaCheck

MediaCheck™ provides an easy way to test and troubleshoot the digital audio and MIDI features of your computer. A series of displays takes you through the testing process step-by-step. If, for some reason, one of the multimedia devices on your computer is not working properly, MediaCheck provides troubleshooting tips to help you get your system up-and-running again.

MediaCheck also provides setup tips for attaching an external MIDI keyboard to your computer — and a video to show you how to make these connections. Once the MIDI cable is installed, you can use MediaCheck's MIDI Input and MIDI Output tests to confirm that your system is operating properly.

When troubleshooting a multimedia computer, it is often necessary to view the sound card drivers if changes need to be made to the drivers' configuration. Locating these drivers can be quite difficult. The Advanced button in MediaCheck calls up SoundCheck,™ an advanced multimedia troubleshooting utility, which displays a detailed listing of all of your computer's sound card drivers. From here you can access the drivers' configuration dialog box and view status information. This tells whether or not the driver is working properly. SoundCheck also provides access to the Windows MIDI and Sound Mapper applications.

MediaCheck Main Screen

Here's an overview of the main screen in MediaCheck. Note that clicking the Advanced button calls up SoundCheck, which takes a more detailed look at your system.

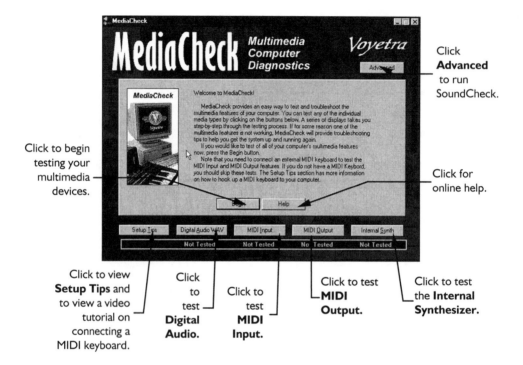

Click **Advanced** to run SoundCheck.

Click to begin testing your multimedia devices.

Click for online help.

Click to view **Setup Tips** and to view a video tutorial on connecting a MIDI keyboard.

Click to test **Digital Audio.**

Click to test **MIDI Input.**

Click to test **MIDI Output.**

Click to test the **Internal Synthesizer.**

Using MediaCheck

With MediaCheck, you can run a complete test of your multimedia devices or individually test specific multimedia functions. For example, you may want to perform a complete test before your run a multimedia application or you may only want to run the MIDI Input Test if you just hooked up an external MIDI keyboard to your PC and want to make certain it is working properly.

Setup Tips

The Setup Tips section includes a video which demonstrates how to connect the MIDI cable to your PC and MIDI keyboard.

To view Setup Tips:

- Click the Setup Tips button located at the bottom of the screen.

 For additional information on connecting your MIDI keyboard to your PC, refer to "Setting Up Your MIDI Keyboard" in the "Up and Running" chapter.

Running the Complete Test

The complete test checks Digital Audio, MIDI Input, MIDI Output, and Internal Synth.

To run the complete test:

1. Click the Begin button on the main screen. MediaCheck automatically takes you step-by-step through the various tests.
2. In each test, you are prompted with questions to help determine that your system is working correctly. Click the appropriate answer for each question.

Running a Specific Test

If you only need to test one function — for example, Digital Audio or MIDI Input or Output — there's no need to run a complete test.

Digital Audio WAV Test

The Digital Audio WAV Test provides a quick check of the digital audio playback capabilities of your multimedia system.

To run the digital audio WAV test:

1. Click the Digital Audio WAV Test button at the bottom of the screen. This will play a digital audio file.
2. When asked if you can hear it, click either Yes or No.
3. Your answer determines the next course of action.
   - If you choose Yes, MediaCheck assumes that your system is functioning properly.
   - If you choose No, MediaCheck suggests several trouble-shooting tips. Try these tips. If one of these works, you should hear the WAV file. If none works, click the Advanced button for more information about your system's WAV drivers.

MIDI Input Test

The MIDI Input Test lets you check that MIDI data is being received from an external source — such as a MIDI keyboard.

To run the MIDI input test:

1. Be sure your MIDI keyboard is connected to your computer.
2. Click the MIDI Input Test button at the bottom of the screen.
3. Click the correct answer for the questions asked.
   - When the keyboard is played, one of the 16 lights should illuminate. For example, if the keyboard is transmitting on MIDI Channel 1, the Channel 1 light illuminates.
   - Each of the 16 lights represents a MIDI input channel. This helps you determine which channel your MIDI keyboard is transmitting on.
   - If none of the MIDI input lights turn on when you play your synth, click the No button and follow the troubleshooting tips.

MIDI Output Test

The MIDI Output Test determines whether MIDI data is being transmitted successfully from your computer to an external source — such as a MIDI synth.

To run the MIDI output test:

1. Be sure your MIDI synth (or other external MIDI device) is connected to your computer.
2. Click the MIDI Output Test button at the bottom of the screen.
3. When asked if you can hear the MIDI file, click Yes or No.
   - If the synth is turned on and connected properly you should hear music coming from the synth.
   - If you cannot hear music playing from the synth, click the No button and follow the troubleshooting tips.

MIDI Drum Sounds

MIDI files transmit their information on different channels, and each channel is usually assigned a different musical instrument sound. Typically drum sounds are fixed to either channel 10 or channel 16. This can sometimes cause a problem.

For example, a game may play a MIDI file with its drum information programmed on channel 16, but the internal synthesizer is set to play its drum sounds on channel 10. This would cause the music to sound strange. Usually the multimedia application provides a way to fix this.

MediaCheck can help by confirming which channel your computer's internal synthesizer has drums mapped to.

Internal MIDI Synthesizer Test

Most multimedia computers have a MIDI synthesizer built in. This enables games and other multimedia applications to play music.

To run the internal MIDI synthesizer test:

1. Click the Internal MIDI Synthesizer Test button. A MIDI file plays a drum part on channel 10.
   - If you hear drums, click Yes and move on to the next test.
   - If you hear a sound like a piano playing a strange melody, click No.

2. When you click No, MediaCheck plays a MIDI drum part on channel 16. If you don't hear anything at this point, there may be a problem with the internal synthesizer in your system or its drivers.

3. Follow the on-screen instructions for information on how to resolve this type of problem.

Test Results

As the test advances, MediaCheck provides feedback. This information appears beneath the test button.

Test Passed   Indicates your system is working correctly.

Test Failed   Indicates your system is not working correctly.

Not Tested   Indicates that test has not been run yet.

Advanced Button

The Advanced button in MediaCheck launches SoundCheck,™ which takes a more detailed look at your multimedia hardware and software. SoundCheck displays all of the sound card drivers currently installed on your system along with the status of each. This information helps determine if there is a problem — such as an address or interrupt conflict — with the hardware or software.

To launch SoundCheck:

- Click the Advanced button at the upper right of the screen.

Do NOT wear headphones when using SoundCheck! Running the tests in SoundCheck can cause sudden volume increases.

SoundCheck Screen

Displays information about the Wave Drivers

Displays information about the MIDI Drivers

Displays information about the CD-ROM Drivers

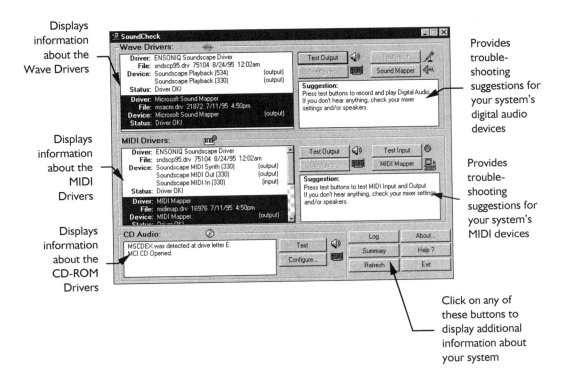

Provides trouble-shooting suggestions for your system's digital audio devices

Provides trouble-shooting suggestions for your system's MIDI devices

Click on any of these buttons to display additional information about your system

Testing Digital Audio

To test digital audio output:

1. Click the Test Output button, in the Wave Drivers section, to play a pre-recorded test file.

2. A dialog box asks whether the file is playing. If there is no sound, check the most likely sources of problems:

   - Speakers are connected incorrectly.

   - Low sound card volume setting .

   - Mute is selected on the sound card's mixer.

   - Speakers or other amplified source is not turned on or the volume setting is too low.

To test digital audio input:

If you are not able to record sound, the problem could simply be bad connections or your drivers may be set up incorrectly. Follow these steps to isolate the problem:

1. Connect a microphone or other device — such as a tape deck — to the appropriate input on your sound card.

2. Use the Mixer utility that came with your Sound Card to select the input device and set the volume level.

3. Click the Test Input button in the Wave Drivers section. The Wave Input Test dialog box opens.

4. Click the Record button.

5. Speak into the microphone for a few seconds — or play a few seconds of the tape.

6. Click the Stop button in the dialog box to stop recording.

7. Click the Play button to hear the results. If you don't hear anything, continue on to Configuring Digital Audio.

Configuring Digital Audio

Before you make any changes to your Wave Driver's configuration, consult your sound card manual.

To configure digital audio:

- Click the Configure button in the Wave Drivers section. SoundCheck displays a dialog box enabling you to change the configuration of the currently-selected driver.

You should change the driver configuration **ONLY** if you have a problem. Most often, you need to restart Windows for any changes to take effect. If you do not restart Windows, click the Refresh button so that SoundCheck can recognize the new configuration.

Testing MIDI Output

To test MIDI output:

- Click the Test Output button in the MIDI Drivers section. The MIDI Output Test dialog box opens. From here you can play a Base Level, Extended Level or Dual Arrangement MIDI test file. This helps determine which MIDI setup is best for your system.

Unless you have selected it for testing, SoundCheck bypasses the MIDI Mapper and sends MIDI data directly to the device driver. This helps you distinguish between incorrect MIDI Mapper settings and problems with the driver software.

Testing MIDI Input

The MIDI Input Dialog Box

To test MIDI input:

- Click the Test Input button in the MIDI Drivers section. This opens the MIDI Test Input dialog box.

MIDI input testing allows you to quickly determine:

- If MIDI data sent from a MIDI device is reaching your computer.
- On which channel MIDI data is being received.

A row of 17 LEDs appears in the MIDI Input dialog box. The first 16 correspond to the 16 MIDI channels; the 17th LED, the one at the far right labeled "Misc," is for non-note MIDI messages that are not channel-specific. As you play a synthesizer or other MIDI device, one or more of the LEDs flash to indicate when MIDI data is being received and on which channel.

MIDI

To configure MIDI:

- Click the MIDI Mapper button to open the Windows MIDI configuration utility.

In Windows 3.1:

- It opens the MIDI Mapper.

In Windows 95:

- It opens the MIDI Properties dialog box.

Use either utility to choose an appropriate setup for your MIDI output device, edit an existing setup or create new ones. As a general guide:

- Base Level synths, typically the earlier FM synthesis sound cards, only use channels 11 through 16, with drums on channel 16.
- Extended Level synths, typically better FM synthesis sound cards, use channels 1 through 10, with drums on channel 10.
- General MIDI synths, typically wavetable synthesis sound cards or external high-end keyboard systems, use all 16 MIDI channels, with drums on channel 10.

Testing CD Audio

A message in the status box in the CD Audio section tells you whether or not MSCDEX was detected. If it is detected, a second message informs you of the status of the Windows MCI CD audio driver. If SoundCheck tells you that MSCDEX was not detected, refer your CD-ROM drive's manual for the proper installation of MSCDEX.

To test CD audio:

1. Place a disc with audio tracks in the CD-ROM drive. Use a commercial CD recording — the kind you buy in a record store.
2. Check your mixer settings. Be sure that the CD-ROM drive is selected and that the volume is turned up enough.
3. Click the Test button to play a CD Audio track.

Summary Button

The Summary screen displays an overview of your system's audio capabilities. You can also run a speed diagnostic of your system from this screen.

Not all sound cards actually play at precisely the same sample rate. Sound-Check can measure how accurate the playback of your sound card is.

At the bottom of this screen is the Wave Sync button. This runs a diagnostic to test the actual sample rates of your sound card.

To run a speed diagnostic of your system:

1. Click the Summary button to open the Audio Capabilities & Related Data screen.
2. Click the Run button to test your system's speed.

Log Button

The Log button opens Notepad and creates a log file containing extensive configuration information.

This file contains data generated during testing that can be useful to you and to tech support people.

Wave Sync

Wave Sync tests your hardware's ability to accurately synchronize digital audio and MIDI.

 It is only necessary to use Wave Sync if you are working with applications that have this option — such as Voyetra's Digital Orchestrator Plus.™

To test Wave Sync:

1. In SoundCheck, click Summary to display the Audio Capabilities & Related Data dialog box. Then click Wave Sync.
2. Choose the Wave Out Device. (This is how sound will be played out of your sound card. Usually you will see the name of the sound card displayed in this box.)
3. Select the Sample Rate to test.
4. Click the Start button.
5. When you are done, also check the Wave In Device by selecting "None" for Wave Out and selecting the sound card for Wave In.

You will notice numbers calculating. Note that this may take a LONG time.

Here's an explanation of the terms used in the Wave Sync test:

Elapsed Time   Is a measure of how much time has passed, in milliseconds, since you clicked the Start button.

Actual Sample Rate   Is the true sample rate of the sound card. As time passes, the accuracy of this number increases. You will be able to see the Actual Sample Rate number begin to stabilize as time goes on.

Deviation   Is the running margin of error that your sound card's drivers may produce.

What the Deviation numbers mean:

Between 0 and 10	Excellent for synching digital audio and MIDI.
Between 11 and 50	Good for synching digital audio and MIDI.
Between 50 and 500	Fair (it may be a bit unstable) for synching digital audio and MIDI.
Over 500	Synching digital audio and MIDI will not work.

Be aware that many sound cards have a very low Wave Out deviation and a high Wave In deviation.

The timing of digital audio playback is handled solely by your sound card driver. If you have a multimedia program that synchronizes digital audio with another function — such as MIDI to WAV — it must ask the sound card exactly where into the playback of the WAV file it is at any moment. This information is gathered by the application communicating with your sound card's WAV driver. This information is then used to calculate at what point the WAV file should sound. If there is a large discrepancy in this number — where the sound is and where the sound card driver thinks it is — the application will not play the sound at the correct moment. This can result in an out-of-sync playback.

Appendix A

Keyboard Lessons' Content

In Keyboard Lessons there are six Sections. Each Section has five Chapters. Each Chapter has a series of Lessons.

Although you can open any of the Lessons at any time, we suggest that you move sequentially through the Lessons, since the content was specifically designed to build from one lesson to the next.

An outline of the content in the Lessons appears on the pages which follow.

 To load Keyboard Lessons, click on the sheet music on the piano in the Piano Room.

Section I: Getting Started, The Right Hand

Chapter 1:
Ready to Play, Learning Note Names
1. Introduction
2. Playing By Ear
3. Five White Notes for the Right Hand
4. The Staff & Clef; Whole Notes
5. Exercises
6. Half Notes & Quarter Notes; Right Hand
7. Our First Song "Ode to Joy"

Chapter 2:
Developing Finger Flexibility
1. Reading Notation
2. Four Bar Tunes
3. Ear Training - Playing by Ear
4. Note Reading Practice
5. Playing Songs
6. Buzzing Bees
7. Jingle Bells
8. Birds Are Back
9. Merrily We Roll Along

Chapter 3:
More Notes to Play
1. Treble Clef White Notes from C to C
2. The C Major Scale
3. Careful Fingering and Numbers
4. Eight Note Melodies
5. Playing Along with the Video

Chapter 4:
Right Hand Stretches
1. Up & Down the Treble Staff
2. Learning About Intervals
3. Interval Exercises
4. Melodies with Intervals
5. Melodies with Scale Passages

Chapter 5:
Playing More New Pieces
1. Playing New Songs
2. Oh, Susanna
3. Blow the Man Down
4. London Bridge
5. Spring Song
6. Sleep, Baby, Sleep

Section 2: Rhythm Training, New Notes

Chapter 1:
Musical Counting & Time Signatures
1. Beats in Music
2. Grouping Beats; Eighth Notes
3. Practice in Counting
4. Counting in Songs
5. Counting 3 Beats in Songs
6. Counting 4 Beats in Songs

Chapter 2:
Rests – Musical Silences
1. Counting Musical Silences
2. Rests & Intervals
3. Rest & More Notes
4. Eighth Rests & Mixed Rests
5. B Below Middle C
6. Counting & Playing

Chapter 3:
Some Black Notes
1. Sharps & Flats
2. Some Challenges
3. Learning B Flat
4. Exercises in Reading F Sharp
5. Exercises in Reading B Flat

Chapter 4: Octaves & Upbeats
1. Octaves
2. Octave Exercise
3. An Octave Melody
4. Upbeats
5. Downbeats

Chapter 5:
Dotted Notes
1. Dotted Half Notes
2. Playing Rounds
3. Dotted Quarter Notes
4. Using Dotted Quarter Notes
5. Two Notes in the Right Hand

Section 3: The Left Hand, Two Hands Together

Section 4: Sharp Keys

Chapter 1:
The Key of G
1. The G Major Scale
2. Key Signatures
3. Left Hand Note Exercises
4. Left Hand Exercises in G
5. Turkey in the Straw

Chapter 2:
The Key of D
1. The D Major Scale
2. Agility Exercises in D
3. Pieces in the Key of D
4. Trumpet Voluntary in D
5. Spring (from the Four Seasons)

Chapter 3:
The Key of A
1. The A Major Scale
2. Finger Exercises in the Key of A
3. Interval Practice in A Major
4. Songs in A Major
5. Flow Gently, Sweet Afton

Chapter 4:
Tied Notes & Naturals
1. Counting Tied Notes
2. Tied Note Songs
3. Tied Notes Across Bar Lines
4. Left Hand Patterns
5. O Sole Mio

Chapter 5:
Playing with Confidence
1. Coordinating the Right & Left Hands
2. Two-Handed Coordination Exercise # 1
3. Playing Naturals
4. Alternating Hands Exercises
5. The Harmonious Blacksmith

Section 5: Flat Keys, Sixteen Notes

Chapter 1:
The Key of F
1. The Key of F
2. The F Major Scale
3. Pieces in the Key of F
4. Piano Concerto # 1
5. Alleluia (by Mozart)

Chapter 2:
The Key of B Flat
1. The B Flat Major Scale
2. Playing the B Flat Major Scale
3. Left Hand Work in B flat
4. Right Hand Work in B Flat
5. A Song in B Flat

Chapter 3:
Sixteenth Notes
1. Sixteenth Notes
2. Sixteenth Note Practice

Chapter 4:
Rhythm Focus
1. Rhythmic Reading Exercises
2. Rhythmic Exercises in Sharp Keys
3. More Left Hand Rhythm Work
4. Rhythmic Exercises in Flat Keys
5. A Famous Tune

Chapter 5:
Wrap-Up
1. Fun Pieces to Play
2. A Soothing Waltz
3. Juliet's Waltz
4. An American Tune
5. Danse Macabre

Section 6: Chords, 6/8 Time

Chapter 1:
Learning Chords
1. Block Chords
2. Block Chords for the Right Hand
3. Playing Chords with Two Hands
4. Playing Chords in Songs
5. Caro Nome

Chapter 2:
Arpeggios
1. Broken Chords for the Left Hand
2. Broken Chords for the Right Hand
3. Arpeggios for Two Hands
4. Comparing Arpeggios with Block Chords
5. Greensleeves with Arpeggio Accompaniment

Chapter 3:
6/8 Time
1. How 6/8 Time Works
2. Pieces in 6/8 Time
3. Marionette March
4. 6/8 Time & Chords
5. De Colores

Chapter 4:
Full Review
1. Arpeggios & Chords
2. Come Back to Sorrento
3. Brahms' Lullaby
4. Waltz in C
5. Melody in F

Chapter 5:
Solo Pieces
1. Can-Can
2. Minuet in G
3. Le Secret
4. Fledermaus Waltz
5. A Little Night Music

Appendix B

Troubleshooting

Fortunately, the situations that cause the most multimedia problems are among the easiest to fix. Start your troubleshooting journey with the general suggestions below. If you still have problems, look up the specific symptoms you're experiencing.

Throughout the troubleshooting process, don't forget another valuable resource — the hardware manuals that came with your sound card or other peripherals.

First, confirm that your sound card is connected to a working output device such as headphones, speakers or an amplifier with speakers. If you are using speakers, make certain that they:

- Are plugged into the correct port on your sound card.
- Are turned on and have the volume set to an adequate level.
- Have their own source of power. Most sound cards can supply enough power for headphones, but not for external speakers. Depending on the type, your speakers will need to be plugged into a wall outlet or an amplifier, or will be powered by batteries.

If the speakers are not the problem, then you will have to check your multimedia devices. To do so, you can use:

- Windows® Media Player
- Voyetra's MediaCheck™

Media Player

There are three devices you can test using the Windows Media Player: the MIDI Sequencer, digital audio (Sound), and Video.

To open the Media Player in Windows 3.1:

1. Double-click the Accessories program group.
2. Double-click the Media Player icon.

To open the Media Player in Windows 95:

1. Click Start.
2. Point to Programs. Point to Accessories. Point to Multimedia.
3. Click Media Player. Media Player opens.

To test multimedia devices with Media Player:

1. Click Device to display the multimedia devices on your system. If you do not see Sound, Video for Windows or MIDI Sequencer listed in the menu, they are not properly installed on your system. Refer to your user's manual or contact your hardware manufacturer for assistance.
2. Click the name of the device — Sound, Video for Windows, or MIDI Sequencer — you want to test.
3. Locate a file of the type of media you want to test and click Open.
4. Click the Play button. If you hear the sound or MIDI or see the video, the drivers are installed and working properly. If any of these multimedia devices fail to operate correctly, contact your hardware manufacturer.

Setting the Mixer

Some of the basic problems that occur with multimedia applications can easily be remedied by checking the Windows 95 mixer. With the mixer, you can control the volume of the different components on your computer's sound system.

Windows 3.1 does not include a mixer, although many sound cards include mixer applications for Windows 3.1. If you are running Windows 3.1, check your sound card's documentation to determine if you have a mixer and how to access it.

To open the mixer in Windows 95:

1. Click Start.
2. Point to Programs. Point to Accessories. Point to Multimedia.
3. Click Volume Control. Make any necessary changes from the Volume Control Panel.

Possible Mixer Problems

❝ The sound is too low or I don't hear any sounds at all. ❞

❝ Some of my components work, but others do not. For example, I can hear MIDI but I cannot hear WAV (digital audio).❞

Possible Problem

The mixer settings are too low or some of the components are muted.

Possible Solution

Check the mixer to make sure all of the components' volumes are at least half way to the top. Also, check that none of the components are muted. In particular, check the Master volume setting if there is one.

❝ MIDI and WAV (digital audio) files do not play simultaneously. ❞

Possible Problem

The sound card cannot support the simultaneous playing of MIDI and WAV.

Possible Solution

Open two instances of Media Player. In one play a MIDI file, in the other play a WAV file. If they do not play simultaneously, contact your sound card manufacturer.

Troubleshooting MIDI

" I can't find the connectors to hook my sound card and my MIDI keyboard together. "

Possible Problem

Your keyboard is not a MIDI device. Not all synthesizers or electronic keyboards support MIDI.

Possible Solution

Look for round MIDI plugs labeled MIDI IN, MIDI OUT or MIDI THRU. They are usually found on the back panel of the MIDI keyboard. If your keyboard is not equipped with these plugs, you will not be able to hook your keyboard to your computer.

Possible Problem

Your sound card did not come with a MIDI connector cable.

Possible Solution

Most sound cards don't have MIDI connectors. A special adapter cable that connects to the joystick port is used instead. The manufacturer of your sound card can probably provide you with one, or you can purchase one from Voyetra.

" I'm getting sound, but it there's interference with it. "

Possible Problem

A hum, hissing or other constant undertone of noise usually indicates electrical interference or a hardware malfunction.

Possible Solution

Increase the sound card's output level and lower the amplifier's volume. If that doesn't help, try it the other way around.

If you are not able to resolve this problem, contact the hardware manufacturer.

❝ I do not hear anything when I play my MIDI keyboard. ❞

Possible Problem

Your sound card isn't connected to an output.

Possible Solution

Be sure your sound card is connected to a working output device such as headphones, speakers or an amplifier with speakers — and that you are using self-powered speakers. The sound card's amp isn't designed to power external speakers.

Possible Problem

Your MIDI cables are not plugged in correctly.

Possible Solution

Make sure that the MIDI cable runs from the MIDI keyboard's MIDI Out to the computer's MIDI In and vice versa.

Possible Problem

Your synthesizer is not set up to transmit MIDI.

Possible Solution

Some MIDI instruments send and/or receive MIDI data automatically, or can be configured to do so. Others require that you take specific steps to transmit MIDI each time you turn on the synthesizer. Check your MIDI instrument's instructions to find out how to set it up to transmit MIDI. The salesperson who sold you the MIDI instrument may also be helpful.

Possible Problem

The MIDI drivers are not properly configured.

Possible Solution

Run MediaCheck to diagnose and fix the problem.

Possible Problem

There is no power to the MIDI keyboard.

Possible Solution

Check to make sure the MIDI keyboard is plugged in and turned on.

Possible Problem

Your synthesizer and software are not set to send and receive on the same MIDI input device.

Possible Solution

Use the MIDI Setup dialog box in Keyboard Lessons to check that it is set to receive on the same MIDI input device that the synth is connected to. You can also use MediaCheck to confirm that MIDI data is being received.

❝ When playing a MIDI file I don't hear anything. ❞

Possible Problem

The MIDI file is an Extended Level file and your sound card is set up for Base Level, or vice-versa.

Possible Solution

Run MediaCheck to help diagnose and resolve the problem.

Possible Problem

The wrong output port is selected in the MIDI Port Setup dialog box.

Possible Solution

Check that the correct MIDI Port is selected in the MIDI Setup dialog box in Keyboard Lessons.

❝ When I play the MIDI keyboard, I hear a strange echo or the notes sound doubled-up — thicker. Sometimes I run out of voices and not all the notes sound. ❞

Possible problem

Your MIDI file contains a Base-Level and an Extended Level arrangement, and you're trying to play both of them at the same time.

Possible solution

Set the MIDI Mapper in Windows 3.1, or the MIDI Configuration in Windows 95, to play only channels 1 through 10, or only channels 13 through 16. MediaCheck can help you determine which option is correct for your situation.

Possible problem

The MIDI data arriving at the MIDI In is echoed to the MIDI Out.

Possible solution

In the MIDI Setup dialog box, try turning MIDI Thru off. If it stops, you've found the problem. If you are using a keyboard controller, try turning the local control off. See the documentation for the keyboard to do this.

❝ It sounds as if tracks are missing from my MIDI file. Also, other parts sound very strange and there are no drum sounds. ❞

Possible Problem

Your MIDI Mapper in Windows 3.1 or the MIDI Configuration in Windows 95 is not set up properly; you're trying to play an Extended-Level arrangement on a Base-Level synth.

Possible Solution

In Windows 3.1, check that the MIDI Mapper is set up correctly for your sound card.

In Windows 95, check that the MIDI configuration is set up correctly for your sound card.

Possible Problem

The file could just be too complex for your synth.

Possible Solution

Edit the file so it doesn't demand as many simultaneous notes and/or instruments from your synth.

Troubleshooting Video

" Videos do not play. "

Possible Problem
Video for Windows is not installed.

Possible Solution
Run SETUPFW.EXE from the VFW directory on the CD.

" I can see the video, but I do not hear any sound. "

Possible Problem
Your mixer is set too low.

Possible Solution
Check the mixer and increase the output volume setting for WAV.

" My video playback skips. "

" The sound and the video are not in sync. "

Possible Problem
Your system is too slow.

Possible Solution
Close any other applications which are open. Also, close any TSRs (Terminate and Stay Resident programs) such as screen savers.

Use a 2x (double-speed) or faster CD-ROM.

Troubleshooting WAV (Digital Audio)

" I cannot hear any digital audio. "

Possible Problem

You do not have the correct drivers installed.

Possible Solution

Check to make sure you have the latest drivers for your sound card. This can be done with MediaCheck.

Run Media Player and test the device labeled Sound. If Sound does not work, contact your sound card manufacturer.

" The sound sometimes stutters and/or stops. "

Possible Problem

Your system may be too slow. The demands of recording and editing digital audio can tax many computer components, particularly older, slower ones.

Possible Solution

Close any open applications.

Check to make sure you have the latest drivers for your sound card.

" The sound is garbled. "

Possible Problem

If sound suddenly stops or "stutters," and/or locks up your computer, you probably have a hardware conflict—more than one device trying to use the same IRQ, I/O address or DMA channel.

Possible Solution

Check your user's manual or contact your hardware manufacturer for help on how to resolve these type of problems.

Appendix C

Technical Support

If you have reviewed the "Troubleshooting" section of this manual, used MediaCheck, and can play a MIDI file and a WAV file with the Windows Media Player, but cannot do so when you are using any of the applications in Teach Me Piano, here's how to contact Technical Support.

- **Voyetra on the Internet**
  E-mail us at support@voyetra.com

- **Voyetra Forum on CompuServe®**
  Type GO VOYETRA at any prompt
  or leave an e-mail message for user ID: 76702.2037

- **Voyetra's Bulletin Board**
  Contact us at 914-966-1216 (any modem speed up to 28,800 baud, 8 bits, 1 stop bit, no parity, ANSI emulation). Post your message or question and we'll answer within a few days. Our Bulletin Board contains useful tips from other users, news about upcoming products and more.

- **Telephone Technical Support**
  For urgent problems, contact Voyetra's Technical Support at 914-966-0600.

Before You Call

- If possible, use a phone near your computer and have the application running.

- We might need to ask about the hardware installed in your system — the sound card, synthesizer, MIDI interface or other devices you are using. Try to have the manufacturer's manuals nearby.

Be prepared to explain what you were doing when the problem occurred and any error messages you received.

 You will need the Product ID number if you phone for Technical Support. You should have written this number on the first page of this manual.

However, if you didn't, this number can be found on the top half of the Registration Card which came with the software or in the About box for Teach Me Piano.

Appendix D

End-User License Agreement

By installing this Software you acknowledge that you have read, understood and agree to abide by the terms and conditions of this Agreement. If you do not agree with the terms of this Agreement, promptly contact the seller of this Software to arrange an appropriate remedy.

SOFTWARE LICENSE: This is a legal agreement (Agreement) between you (either an individual or an entity) and Voyetra Technologies (Voyetra) that sets forth the license terms and conditions for using the enclosed software (Software) and updates of the Software. In this Agreement, the term "Use" means loading the Software into RAM, as well as installing it onto a hard disk or other storage device.

The Software is owned by Voyetra and is protected under United States copyright laws as well as international treaty provisions. You must treat the Software as you would any other copyrighted material. Voyetra retains title and ownership of the Software. The purchase price for the Software grants you a non-exclusive license to use one copy of the Software on a single computer. You may make copies of the Software solely for archival purposes. You may not make copies of any written material accompanying the Software. You may not allow third parties to use the Software by time-sharing, networking or any other form of multi-user participation. You may not rent, sell, lease, sub-license, time-share or lend the Software to a third party or otherwise transfer this License without written permission from Voyetra. You may not decompile, disassemble, reverse-engineer or modify the Software.

This Agreement is effective until terminated by the destruction of the Software — all of the CD-ROMs and/or diskettes — and documentation provided in this package, together with all copies, tangible or intangible. If you fail to comply with any of the terms and conditions of this Agreement, this License will be terminated and you will be required to immediately return to Voyetra the Software — CD-ROMs and/or diskettes — and documentation provided in this package, together with all back-up copies. The provisions of this Agreement which protect the proprietary rights of Voyetra will continue in force after termination.

LIMITED LIABILITY: You assume responsibility for the selection of the Software to achieve your intended results, and for the installation, use and results obtained from the Software.

VOYETRA MAKES NO REPRESENTATIONS OR WARRANTIES WITH REGARD TO THE SOFTWARE AND DOCUMENTATION, INCLUDING BUT NOT LIMITED TO THE IMPLIED WARRANTIES OF MERCHANTABILITY AND FITNESS FOR A PARTICULAR PURPOSE.

Voyetra shall not be liable for errors or omissions contained in the Software or manuals, any interruption of service, loss of business or anticipatory profits and/or for incidental or consequential damages in connection with the furnishing, performance or use of these materials. The Software and documentation are sold AS IS.

This Limited Warranty gives you specific legal rights and you may also have other rights which vary from state to state. Some states do not allow the limitation or exclusion of implied warranties or of consequential damages, so the above limitations or exclusions may not apply to you. You agree that this is the complete and exclusive statement of the Agreement between you and Voyetra which supersedes any proposal or prior agreement, oral or written, and any other communications between us regarding the subject matter of this Agreement. This Agreement shall be construed, interpreted and governed by the laws of the State of New York, except the federal laws which govern copyrights and registered trademarks. If any provision of this Agreement is found unenforceable, it will not affect the validity of the balance of this Agreement, which shall remain valid and enforceable according to its terms.

Index

O

Online help · iii, 16
Online tutorials
  Connecting the MIDI Cable · 13

P

Page Down · 18
Page Turn Anticipation
  Performance Options dialog box ·
    37
Page Up · 18
Perform video
  Performance Options dialog box ·
    37
Performance Options
  Keyboard Lessons · 31
Performance Options dialog box
  Keyboard Lessons · 36
Performance screen · 30, 36, 53
  using · 54
Performing a piece · 36
Piano Room · 16
Pitch, practicing · 34
Pitches and Clefs · 19
Playing a keyboard instrument
  preparing to play · 22
  proper hand position · 22
Pop-Up menu · iii
Practice
  Evaluation screen · 38
Printer icon · 36
Printing a musical score · 36
Printing a song
  note names and finger numbers · 54
  Songbook · 54
PrintScreen · 18
Product ID number · iii, 17, 88
Progress report
  printing · 43

Progress Screen · 30, 43

Q

Quantizing MIDI files · 37, 52

R

Range icon · 41
Range Selection dialog box · 41
Readme file · 10
Refresh · 63
Registering Your software · ii
  benefits of · 2
Replay My Version
  Evaluation screen · 38
Rhythm
  practicing · 34
Rhythm and pitch
  practicing · 35
Rhythms · 19
Right arrow · 18
Right-click pop-up menu · 17
Running the software · 11

S

See It
  CTRL+Enter · 34
See It icon · 33, 34
Shortcut keys
  Windows · 14
Show note names · 37
Solo · 37
  Performance Options dialog box ·
    37
Songbook · 5, 15, 46
  Composer Tab · 48
  Delete from List · 47
  deleting files from · 50

MIDI · 81
mixer problems · 80
setting the mixer · 79
using Media Player · 78
video · 85